# The Cistercian Way

## A South Lakeland Walk

The Official Guide
by Ian O. Brodie

Carnegie Press, 1989

# Contents

The Cistercian Way
by Ian O. Brodie

Copyright, text and maps © Ian O. Brodie

Published by Carnegie Press, 125 Woodplumpton Road, Cadley, Preston PR2 2LS
with the help and support of South Lakeland and Barrow District Councils

Typeset and layout by Carnegie Press
Printed by T. Snape and Co. Ltd., Bolton's Court, Preston.

First Edition, June 1989.

**ISBN 0 948789 31 X**

# Foreword

I feel that what was once 'Lancashire north of the Sands', or the district of Furness, is the best part of the county of Cumbria – but then I would. I have lived in it for most of my life. Its ancient links with the main part of Lancashire was with the roads across the sands from Lancaster and Hest Bank to Grange and Cartmel, and Cark to Conishead and Dalton; perilous journeys without guides. The guides, until the Dissolution, were monks and there could be none better; for the Augustinians at Cartmel and Conishead Priories, and the Cistercians at the large and powerful Furness Abbey must have crossed and recrossed the sands constantly. And, as the monks controlled the commerce, the coast-side tracks and paths between must surely have been originally of their making. So Ian Brodie appropriately calls the itinerary he has shaped for the explorer of this quite remarkable and attractive Furness landscape that he and I enjoy so well, "The Cistercian Way".

There is much delightfully unspoilt natural beauty to savour and much to excite botanists, geologists and ornithologists here. But if the spirits of the monks and canons stalk these tracks and paths and byways there are others too of the Furness folk who have left their mark in the places of interest: miners and mariners and merchantmen, smelters and smiths, fishermen and shipbuilders; the engineers and entrepreneurs of the Industrial Revolution. Many of the marks are mere memories; dim brush marks on a unique canvas.

All this and more; there is much to savour on an unhurried journey along this "Cistercian Way".

*John Wyatt,*
*Spring, 1989*

# The Cistercian Way

## Introduction

The Cistercian Way covers some 55 kilometres (33 miles) from Grange-over-Sands to Barrow-in-Furness or vice versa. Not only is there much delectable countryside to pass through but the route has been chosen to link together many places of interest which the visitor to the area – be they on foot, as this book intends, on cycle, or using other forms of transport – should find interesting.

The major attraction, besides the countryside, is Furness Abbey and this, through its Cistercian Order of monks, gave rise to the title of the walk. However, this is not to belittle the other religious and historical sites passed en route.

The walk could be done in easy stages using the Furness Line trains or bus services or could easily be covered by the keen, head-down rambler in a couple of days, tides permitting. However, to rush would be to miss too much of interest.

To help the walker, the two District Councils through which the route passes, South Lakeland and Barrow-in-Furness Borough, have produced a leaflet to promote the route and to provide information about accommodation and, hopefully, a reduced rate entrance ticket to all the payable sites along the route will be possible. The two councils have adopted the route as part of their tourism strategy for the Cartmel and Furness peninsulas and have taken action to ensure that the walk is suitably free from obstruction and is waymarked. The leaflets concerned can be obtained from the various Tourist Information Centres operated by those councils and a list of their addresses is given at the end of the book. These centres also offer a free booking service for accommodation for the walk.

This introduction outlines the route and the various options and logistical problems in choosing when alternatives are possible. The walker who proposes to cross the Leven Sands or from Piel to Walney must pay attention to the essential information in these sections.

The main text details the route description, along with sketch maps and information on places of interest along the way. Ordnance Survey 1:25 000 sheets SD 16/26; 17/27 and 37/47 will also need to be carried.

The walk begins, or ends, at Grange-over-Sands railway station and links in with most other stations between there and Barrow-in-Furness and it is thus possible to do the walk in stages. However the route is ideally walked in around four days or so – depending on the interests of the walker.

From Grange the route goes via woodlands to Hampsfell, which, at 220 metres, is the highest part of the route. The way then descends to Cartmel, with its Priory, before continuing to Cark by way of Holker Hall.

From Cark the coast of the Leven Estuary is easily reached but unless you intend to cross the sands to Chapel Island and Conishead Priory, you may go by train from here to Ulverston.

Ulverston itself is a pleasant market town. The villages of Great and Little Urswick, with their prehistoric associations, are next. The route then goes to Furness Abbey by way of Dalton and its small castle. From the Abbey the way is by small villages to the coast at Roa Island and the romantic setting of the castle on Piel Island. Barrow is then reached by the first few miles of the Cumbria Coastal Way or, tides and choice permitting, via Walney Island.

It is hoped to extend the walk from Cark to Ulverston around the head of the Leven Estuary for those who prefer not to cross the sands. However, this will involve the creation of new footpaths and will not be available for a few years.

Appendices of useful addresses and contact telephone numbers, including the Tourist Information Centres, and a bibliography follow at the end of the volume.

# Acknowledgements

In compiling this walk I have to thank both South Lakeland and Barrow Borough Councils for their commitment and assistance in preparing the route. Additionally, Colin Speakman of Transport for Leisure and Jennifer Snell of Ulverston have given invaluable advice. Mrs Noble of Swarthmoor Hall and Mr Pye of the nearby Friends Meeting House, the staff of Holker Hall, the people of Conishead Priory, Linda McBride of Glaxo, Mrs Gill Richardson and last – but in many ways foremost – the Sand Pilot of the Leven Sands, Alf Butler, have all rendered invaluable service in producing this book.

*Ian O. Brodie*
*January, 1989.*

Stage One

# Grange-over-Sands – Hampsfell – Cartmel

*5 kilometres (3 miles).*

Grange-over-Sands is a good place to start because it is served by rail, whilst bus and car travellers can easily reach it from the M6 via the A590. Cars can be parked temporarily near the station in Windermere Road or at the station if you intend to use the train at the end of a day's stage.

SKETCH MAP 1 and SD 37/47.

*From the station go foward, with the ornamental gardens and famous duck pond on your left, to the garage and right into Windermere Road. Follow the left hand pavement until it ends at a footpath sign (Hampsfield – which is the correct name of Hampsfell).*

*Use this path, which climbs gradually through Eggerslack Wood and is well signed, until it emerges on the open fell through a stile in the wall. A short Nature Trail Guide, in need of revision, can be purchased in Grange railway station to accompany you on this first part of the walk. The way through the wood crosses a track and at the second such crossing go slightly left. Ignore all side tracks but make sure you keep to the left branch just before the stile in the wall.*

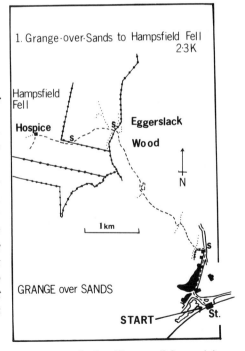

1. Grange-over-Sands to Hampsfield Fell
2·3K

The walk is largely over that ring of attractive Carboniferous (Mountain) Limestone which once covered the Lakes but now incompletely encircles it – the product of warm, shallow seas and the shells and skeletal remains of tiny sea creatures some 280 million years ago. The rock gives rise to a flora very different from the central Lake District, and lime loving plants add an extra dimension to the walk not only in increasing the number of species to be seen but also because they are so abundant. Eggerslack Wood and the open top of Hampsfell provide only an introduction to the flora – take your flower book with you for identifying these. Eggerslack Wood is owned by the Forestry Commission, yet for the most part it is still a wood of natural species, in that alien conifers do not dominate. Yew gives darkness to the wood, yet it adds colour all year round.

*With your back to the stile follow the track onto open land and after a few strides, keeping to the right of an overhead wire pole, pass between two trees with a cairn and then continue upwards towards the left hand wall which you will meet at a stile some 30m before the top corner of the wall. Follow the wall when over the stile and when it bends away to the right climb the fell ahead and the famous shelter, the Hampsfell Hospice, soon comes into view.*

# Hampsfield Fell Hospice

The Hospice was provided by a pastor of Cartmel last century for the "shelter and entertainment of travellers over the fell". The well-built stone structure has an exterior flight of steps to the flat roof viewpoint, which is complete with indicator, and a Greek inscription. Inside is a well worded notice, in the form of a riddle and its answer, in verse which would appeal both to vandals and to those of a literary disposition.

After you have tried to solve the riddle inside, you can enjoy the extensive views of the Lakes, Yorkshire Dales and seaward Lancashire with the aid of the viewfinder on top, as well as more local views of the Kent Estuary and Morecambe Bay. The views are indeed magnificent and a clear day adds much to the character of the walk and rewards the effort of the short climb. The monks of Cartmel are said to have bred horses and Hampsfell was one area where they grazed.

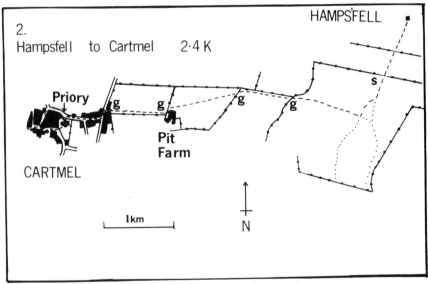

SKETCH MAP 2 and SD 37/47.

*From the shelter continue your walk in the direction of Morecambe Bay, more particularly aim to the right of Heysham Nuclear Power Station and the peninsula that holds Humphrey Head. Go down to the wall to find a path and stile.*

*Over the stile follow the distinct track ahead and, when it comes towards the dip, bear right, cross the dip and descend on a narrower path that leads in the direction of Cartmel with its priory and backdrop of Mount Barnard (the curious treed knoll) with the Level Estuary and Chapel Island beyond.*

*Go down, with the overhead wire pole on your right, to meet a kissing gate in the wall across your way. Pass through, follow the right hand wall to a signed gate and, in the following field, go to pass the right hand side of the farm buildings.*

*Behind the buildings is a gate and stile. In the field beyond follow the left*

*hand boundary over the hillock to meet a gate and short enclosed path between
the houses. On the road go left but then turn right to reach the churchyard by
an outlying part of Cartmel village. Go through the yard to the front gate.*

## Cartmel and its priory

A full exploration of the village and the Priory, with its unique tower, is strongly
recommended. According to legend, the site of the original monastery was to
have been Mount Barnard – a place we shall soon pass on the walk. However, St
Cuthbert appeared in a vision to the monk's architect and ordered that it be built
between two springs flowing in opposite directions. The monk began work in
such a location on the hillside; next morning, however, he found his foundation
blocks cast in a field below. This was where the two springs were to be found and
it is where the church still stands today. One author claims that the monks also
built a small chapel to St Bernard on the hill.

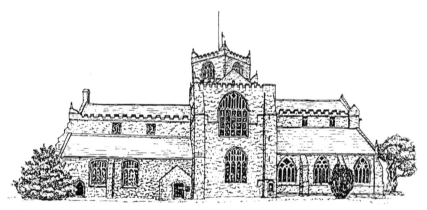

The link with St Cuthbert arises, as William Palmer records, because he was
given the land of Cartmel by King Egfrith of Deira in 686 in order to enlighten
the Britons of that far-flung region. Cartmel Priory was founded by William
Mareschal (Marshall), Baron of Cartmel and Earl of Pembroke, in around 1188
for Canons Regular of St Augustine, and was dedicated to St Mary. With it
Marshall endowed all the Cartmel land, which extended northwards to the east
side of Windermere, and some lands in Ireland. Marshall was later Protector for
the boy Henry III and helped rescue England from the French.

Cartmel was never a very wealthy house and the building period was
prolonged. By the end of the fourteenth century the unstable cloisters were
totally replaced and around this time, during the early fifteenth century, the nave
and diagonal belfry were probably erected.

Now, nothing can be seen of the priory except the church itself and a
gatehouse in the village square. The destruction at the time of the Dissolution, in

1537, was thorough, the Earls of Derby and Sussex acting as Henry VIII's Commissioners. The lands were confiscated, all metals were stripped from the buildings, including the lead from the church roof, and the summary destruction of the church itself was only prevented by the production of documentary evidence that the founder had stipulated that an altar and a priest should be provided for the people. Indeed, unlike the Furness Cistercians, the Augustinians of Cartmel had allowed the local people to worship in the Priory Church. The Commissioners appealed for guidance and were told that, because the laws were directed towards the dissolution of monasteries, not parish churches, so a portion of the church, the south aisle, could be preserved for the use of the parish. The rest of the church was in a bad state and open to the weather until in 1620, a benefactor, George Preston of Holker, with help from parishoners, began restoration. The church was roofed, and the very fine Renaissance screens of richly carved black oak and stall canopies were presented by the benefactor. Further necessary restoration was carried out in the 1850s by the seventh Duke of Devonshire after the building was found to be in very poor condition and an extensive period of restoration begun in 1837.

Because it was largely built in a transitionary architectural period, and has been altered since, the church contains a variety of styles. The great east window, of Caen stone, dates from the middle of the fifteenth century; the surviving medieval glass, including the Virgin and Child and John the Baptist, was cleaned and reset in 1964. Some other glass, removed at the Dissolution, was installed in St Martin's in Bowness. In the middle of the fifteenth century work on the tower and nave was done, but the fact that the nave is short and built with irregular stones might suggest that funds were short.

Tom Clare's book *Archaeological Sites of the Lake District* has a few pages of notes about the Priory structure and architecture. He also covers the gatehouse in the village square. The book also proves useful later in the walk at Dalton Castle and, more particularly, Furness Abbey.

The main entrance porch to the church dates from 1626 but the doorway dates to around 1200 and has a carved semi-circular head. Dog-tooth moulding can be seen above the north door. Inside, to the left, is the short 15th-century nave and, in its south-west corner, is the original door called the 'Cromwell Door' which gets its name from local tradition that the holes in it were used by the parishioners to fire at Cromwellian soldiers. During a restoration, fragments of lead were found in the holes. A modern sculpture by Lakeland artist Josephina de Vasconcellos, 'They Fled by Night', adorns the nave. In the north-west corner is the memorial to Lord Frederick Cavendish who was assassinated in Pheonix Park in Dublin in 1882. In the north transept (early 13th-century) can be seen the church's only Early English window. The crossing retains four original piers. The brass chandelier was presented in 1734.

The arch into the Piper Choir (north east of the crossing) is oddly formed, of Gothic shape but bearing Norman chevron moulding. Only in the Piper Choir (the opposite side is the Town Choir) is the original roof intact. The Noble Choir, from the thirteenth century, has some superb carved misericords, of humour and imagination, and include a mermaid with two tails, a hedgehog, an ape doctor, several grotesque figures, some religious carvings and some intricate foliage work.

The windows were replaced in the fifteenth century and the three figures are probably an Archbishop of York, The Virgin and Child and St John the Baptist. The east window has suffered from the heavy hand of the Victorians. The screens were replaced in 1620 and are probably of Flemish craftsmanship.

The oldest intact tomb is of the first Lord Harrington (d. 1347) and his wife. Sir John, of that family, is credited with ridding the district of a dangerous man-eating wolf from a cave above the spa well on nearby Humphrey Head. Other versions of the story refer to this as the last wolf in England. The south transept belongs to the original building and the large windows were inserted in the fifteenth century but contain Victorian glass.

Several graves mark those who perished on the sands crossings, including that of a young man and his mother who drowned at the same spot but at different times. The grave of William Taylor, the teacher of William Wordsworth, is also to be found.

A once stolen copy of Spenser's *Faerie Queen* (1596 first edition) is owned by the church. Copies of Fox's *Book of Martyrs* (1610), a Basle Bible (1502) and a volume by Thomas Aquinas (1509) are also in the collection.

The tower, of massive construction, is Norman to the level of the transept roof with the upper tower built diagonally across it some 200 years later.

The gatehouse in the centre of the village (possibly mid fourteenth-century and now owned by the National Trust), was also part of the Priory. The upper floor was used as a grammar school in the seventeenth and eighteenth centuries and is now a craft shop. The nearby obelisk is eighteenth century in date. The second-hand bookshop and craft galleries around and near the square can be visited before continuing towards the racecourse at the far western side of the village. Several village pubs and other establishments offer food.

Stage Two

# Cartmel – Holker – Leven Estuary
*7.5 kilometres (4 miles)*

## Route Choice A

*Starting at the near right hand side of the car park on Cartmel Race Course, at the far end of the village from the Priory, there is a footpath sign on the right by a gateway. Follow the path over the land in the middle of the race course by keeping to the left hand side of the cricket square, and pass through a stile in the rails to cross the far side of the course track and enter a wood.*

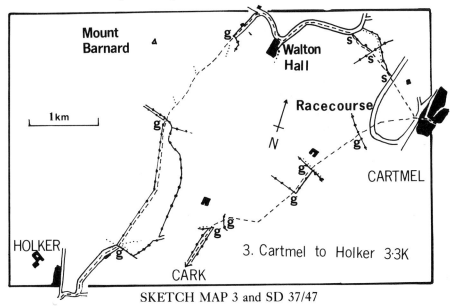

SKETCH MAP 3 and SD 37/47

Underfoot in the wood are rocks of the Silurian series. They are darker and older than the Carboniferous limestone which we meet on most of the walk.

*Climb up the most obvious path through the trees and bear left at the fork after the steep climb to leave the wood by a gap stile. Follow the right hand wall through the field to emerge on a road by a further gap stile. Turn left on the road, pass Walton Hall Farm and come to a sign for High Mill House and a footpath sign to Mount Barnard.*

This sign is somewhat misleading, as the top of this 'Mount' is out of bounds. This distinctive knoll is the site where, as we have seen, the monks of Cartmel had originally intended to build their monastery.

*The track bends left to pass a bungalow and house before a gate, with its typical Holker Estates cautionary sign, admits you to the wood. Take the obvious track that climbs across the hillside and eventually levels before descending slightly to a further gate which you use to leave the wood.*

*In the field follow the track by the right hand wall all the way down to a gate and cattle-grid with views of Morecambe Bay ahead. Go over the cattle-grid ignoring the plethora of tracks and paths and go down the enclosed lane to the B5278 road near Holker Hall.*

*Go left, using the pavement to pass the entrance to Holker Hall and Park.*

# Holker Hall

If you intend to use this visit to see the hall, gardens and park, please note they are closed on Saturdays in the open season (Easter Sunday to the last Sunday in October). 10.30 - 6.00 are the opening hours.

The Hall is the home of Mr and Mrs Hugh Cavendish and was the former home of the Dukes of Devonshire, from whom the present owners are descended. As well as the house there are gardens, a 120 acre deer park, the Lakeland Motor Museum, a craft and country museum, guided discovery walks, an adventure playground, a baby animal house and, quite naturally, a cafeteria. Despite all this commercial activity, however, the house and grounds retain their atmosphere of domestic tranquility.

The Hall was originally built in the 16th Century by the Preston family. By inheritance it passed through the Lowther to the Cavendish families and has never been sold. The land came from Cartmel Priory on the Dissolution when it was annexed by the Duchy of Lancaster. The Prestons, a local landholding family, bought the land from the Bishopric of Chester, who had received it from the Duchy. The first house was built in 1604, but was lost temporarily when the son had his estates sequestered because he had dared to entertain some Royalist troops – he had to purchase it back! The Lowthers gained the estate by marriage and then added to the house through the construction of a north wing and the laying out of extensive formal gardens. The estate passed to the Cavendish branch of the family in 1756.

Further extensions and alterations were made in the eighteenth and early nineteenth centuries but in 1871 the entire west wing and much of its contents were destroyed in a fire. Paintings and books of value were among the items lost. The 7th Duke engaged Paley and Austin to rebuild the wing on an even grander scale using red sandstone in an 'Elizabthan' style.

The principal rooms seen in the tour include the library, with over 3,500 volumes, including some from Chatsworth. They include works by the scientist, Henry Cavendish, whose microscope can be seen in the room. Near the doorway, the light switches are hidden behind imitation books with humorous titles. The drawing, billiard and dining rooms are then visited before ascending the elegant stairway. The Wedgewood Bedroom and Dressing Room, Queen Mary's Bedroom, the (7th) Duke's Bedroom, the Gloucester Bedroom and Dressing Room and the Long Gallery are the main rooms. The Hall is the other room on the tour.

The gardens, a 23 acre pleasure ground, make a splendid foil to the house. A well illustrated guide book is available.

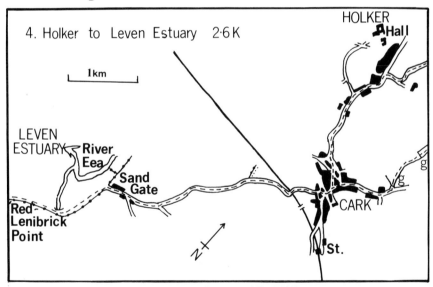

SKETCH MAP 4 and SD 37/47

*Continue along the road following the signs towards Flookburgh until the road crosses the River Eea. Carry on to the station if you intend to use the train to return to Grange or cross to Ulverston (see Stage Three).*

## Route Choice B  (see sketch map 3)

*Follow the track that goes through the car park on Cartmel Race Course and then crosses the course to a gate. Follow the distinct track across the field to the left of the buildings to a further gate.*

*After this an enclosed track leads to a wood with gates to enter and exit. On leaving the wood go up the track to a double gate on your left from where a tarmacadamed track leads above Low Bank Side Farm and, via a further gate, reaches the road on the outskirts of Cark.*

SKETCH MAP 4 and SD 37/47

*Turn right to go into village, passing Cark Hall on your right, and bear left at the road junction to join the Flookburgh road. Descend to where it crosses the River Eea. Continue left down the Flookburgh road for the station.*

ROUTES A and B REJOIN (SKETCH MAP 4 and SD 37/47)

*Go over bridge and immediately turn right to the Engine Inn. Almost at once go left in front of The Fold (fp sign Sandgate) to follow an enclosed path over a superb railway bridge and, with excellent views of Coniston Fells and Leven Estuary, down to a road. Go right to reach the saltmarsh at Sandgate where the bay shrimpers leave their nets and trailers.*

# Fisherfolk of the Bay

The fisherfolk of Flookburgh catch flukes, cockles and shrimps at various seasons from the sands of Morecambe Bay. At one time they took their nets out onto the sands with horse drawn carts; now the remaining few take the carts hauled by tractor.

Shrimps usually are caught from March until the first frosts. A local co-operative boils the shrimps for market and Morecambe Bay shrimp is renouned as a fine local delicacy. However, catches vary from year to year. Fluke, or flounder, also disappear with the frosts.

Bird life is also a feature of the estuary, with oystercatchers and many waders among the sights. Winter sees many birds feeding on the productive mudflats before they return north to breed the following summer. Cedric Robinson's books are ideal reading before embarking on walks in the area.

Stage Three

# Crossing the Leven Estuary
### *3 Kilometres (2 miles)*

At present, there are two possible ways of crossing from the Cark area to Ulverston. It is hoped that in future years an all-season way around the estuary via Greenodd will also be possible.

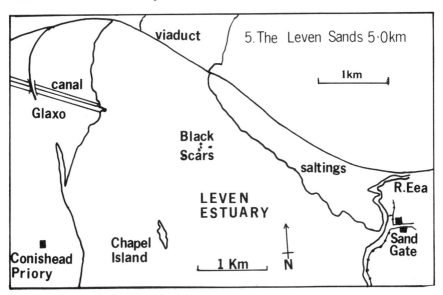

SKETCH MAP 5 and SD 37/47

## ROUTE A

*Take the train from Cark-in-Cartmel to Ulverston.*

Travelling by rail is hardly challenging for the walker. Nevertheless, interesting views of the estuary are obtained from the train – and from Autumn to late Spring it is the only safe way.

ROUTE B

*From Sand Gate walk across the sands to Chapel Island and then come ashore near Conishead Priory.*

Before attempting the sands crossing, phone the sand pilot, Alf Butler, on Ulverston (0229) 54156 and remember the basic rules:

- avoid in winter months (roughly Oct–April);
- consult a tide table, and aim to start on the sands about 4 to 6 hours after the tide has ebbed, the actual time depending on the tide height and wind strength and direction;
- there is a three or four hour window, depending on the tide, in which to cross safely before the turning tide will affect the route. This gives you plenty of time for the crossing and a short visit to Chapel Island;
- remember that tide tables are GMT not BST;
- avoid the sands after periods of heavy or sustained rainfall.

*From Sandgate turn left to follow the coastline path until the reddish cliffs of Lenibrick Point are reached. Cross the estuary from here – having first checked with the guide as to the best route on the day as this can alter. Chapel Island lies easily in view. After Chapel Island make westwards, via the Leven Channel (which is usually on this side of the island but not always so) to come ashore by the wood beneath Conishead Priory.*

*Above: Sand pilot, Alf Butler, there to ensure that walkers cross the perilous Morecambe Sands safely.*

## Chapel Island

Knapp-Fisher describes Chapel Island as the ". . . ancient shrine and seat of a monk or priest who succoured and prayed for those in peril on the sands". He continues that the chapel was ". . . well set up less than 150 years ago as 'ancient ruins' to add beauty to the natural site as was the fashion, the wall with lancet windows and a circular window on Chapel Island, is on the very foundations of a chapel originally founded centuries ago by the monks of Conishead Priory. The island was undoubtedly a resting-place for the Furness monks when they crossed the estuaries to their fisheries."

According to West's *Antiquities of Furness*, the Conishead monks used to say mass for travellers on Chapel Island, which he describes as a small rocky knoll in the Ulverston Sands, about a mile from Bardsea shore. Unfortunately, the tradition has little evidence behind it and, according to Norman Nicholson's *Greater Lakeland*, the building which you see is "that of a mock ruin set up by Colonel Braddyll who built the Gothic-revival Conishead Priory in the early nineteenth century", thus reinforcing Knapp-Fisher's story.

West, however, was very adamant – "In crossing Leven sands to Furness, the chapel isle stands on the left. There, in former times, divine service was performed, at a convenient hour, for such as crossed the sands with the morning tide. The shell of the chapel remains." Evidence tends to confirm that the ruins are a folly – indeed, the island was originally called Harlside and only became Chapel Island in more recent times.

The island, being made of limestone, served as a quarry for the iron smelting industry in earlier centuries. Why they used the island when this part of the mainland is also limestone is unclear.

By walking the sands route you are in good historical company. The monks of Conishead and Furness came this way, as did both John Wesley and George Fox. Early tourists and guidebook writers used the route, as did Robert Bruce's Scots army and the troops of Lambert Simnel (see Furness Abbey and Piel Island later).This way was essential, therefore, to invaders, drovers and tourists alike.

So busy and so treacherous were the sands that the monks created the posts of Guides to the Kent Sands and the Leven Sands. The monks were responsible for the guides (called Carters) until the Dissolution of the Monasteries, whereupon the duty fell to the Duchy of Lancaster, who still have some responsibilities in this direction. The service is managed by a small group of trustees and on the infrequent occasions when a replacement guide is needed, they are usually selected from among the local fishing community. A meagre sum is paid to the guide but a rent-free cottage does go with the job.

In the times prior to the railways, the coaches came from Lancaster via the Keer and Kent Sands and came ashore at Kents Bank or near the Guides House on the outskirts of Grange. They then travelled overland via Allithwaite, Wraysholme Tower (once near the shore itself), to Flookburgh. Up to 1860 this village was the major stopping place between Lancaster and Ulverston. From here the coaches went westwards to Sand Gate but from the early 19th century they went to Cark to avoid the small hill between Flookburgh and the coast. It was from Sand Gate and Cark that they crossed the Leven Sands to Conishead or to the Guide's House at Canal Foot.

Hindle records that the three mile crossing of the Leven often caused more problems that the longer Keer-Kent estuaries. He states that guides recommended travellers not to stand still or the sand under carriage wheels would be washed away. The railway line which took away the sands traffic was completed in 1857.

*Above: Conishead Priory*

Stage Four

# Conishead Shore – Conishead – Ulverston
### *8 kilometres (5 miles)*

SKETCH MAP 6 and SD 37/47

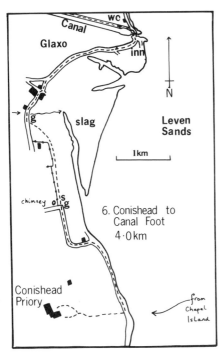

6. Conishead to
Canal Foot
4·0 km

*Coming ashore at Beach Wood, below Conishead Priory, there is a short length of stone wall, behind which a path leads through the wood to Conishead Priory.*

## Conishead Bank

According to Alfred Fell's *The Early Iron Industry of Furness and District*, the oldest reference to one of the local industries is found in a grant, by William de Lancaster III (1220-46), to the Prior of Conishead, of land for a forge, a mine and dead wood to burn coals. Conishead Bank, where we have come ashore, was, in the eighteenth century, a place for shipping iron ore from nearby mines.

It was also the place where the ancient road from Cartmel came ashore, as it was then the only place where cliffs and peat mosses allowed easy access to the land. The track then crossed the Furness peninsula; although some refer to it as a Roman road, the metalled surfaces are probably medieval in date and one section over the marshy Goldmire valley has been described as a typical Bronze Age 'corduroy' road of logs.

## Conishead Priory

Conishead was originally founded as a hospital by the Augustinians but details are unfortunately scarce. The existing house was built as a private residence in 1821 but later became a hydro (with a branch railway linking it to Ulverston opened in 1874), then a Durham Miners Convalescent Home and more latterly an institute for Buddhist studies. The Gothic Revival house was built for Colonel Braddyll and designed by Phillip Wyatt, when the cross bay route was still the main route to the booming industries of western Cumbria.

The site of the priory underlies the house and was originally founded by Gamel de Pennington during the twelfth century as a hospital for relief of 'the poor, decrepit, indigent and lepers', shortly afterwards becoming a priory of Augustinian Canons. About 1180 William de Lancaster, Baron of Kendal and Lord of the Manor of Ulverston under Furness Abbey, granted to the Priory all Conishead, the church at Ulverston, and forty acres in its fields, a salt works and the rights of turbary, pasture, pannage and timber taking in his woods of Furness and the Manor of Ulverston – a grant probably replacing the earlier one by Gamel de Pennington.

From time to time the Priory had various gifts of land and there is evidence of legal wrangles and friction between this house and Furness, settlements of such disputes often going the way of the larger Furness Abbey. We do not know exactly when the hospital ceased. Until the Dissolution in 1536, the priors of Conishead had to maintain the guides over the Leven Sands. After the closure of the priory, the prior was given the vicarage of Orton and the 7 canons a pension of £1 17s 8d each. At sale the priory goods brought £333 (Cartmel only brought £275).

The current house is dominated by two towers over 30m high with a traceried window below showing the principal benefactors of the original Priory. After its use as a miners convalescent home it fell into disrepair before being taken over by the Manjushri Institute as a centre for Tibetan Buddhist studies. In spite of scarce financial resoures, they have largely repaired the damage suffered during the neglect. The house and grounds are a fine testament to the work done and both can be visited. A guide book is available which sets out information on the house, its history, the story of its saving and restoration, its woods and grounds and about its Buddhist community. The house can, and should, be visited.

The Braddylls, who had Conishead built in 1821, were originally a Lancashire family that moved to the Ulverston area from over the sands. John Braddyll had purchased Whalley Abbey from the Crown. His grandson, also called John, received a commission to survey the Queen's woods in Furness, thus apparently beginning the family connection with Furness.

During the years of the Romantics in the last century, a small cell was built in the grounds of the house and a man was paid to act as a hermit! The hermitage can be seen on the hillock above Conishead Priory. The hermit was not allowed to cut his toe nails or hair and was there to be 'poked' by Bradyll's guests.

For up to date information on opening days and times, telephone Ulverston 54029.

SKETCH MAP 6 and SD 37/47.

*Retrace your steps to the shore, go left along the estuary side path towards the slag bank with Coniston Old Man peering above. Keep by the shore until the shingle gives way to a track and then, by a cottage that stands where the railway crossing once was, follow the now metalled lane that leads inland.*

*Follow the lane until it bends left near a lone chimney that once belonged to a wireworks.*

When the works were demolished the chimney was left standing as a beacon for shipping on the Leven coming to the Ulverston iron works.

*Leave the metalled road and go straight ahead by a gate and stile. Over the stile the path goes along the raised bank parallel to the slag heap. After the parallel left hand boundary bends away go across the field to the left of the overhead wire pole to reach a gate and kissing gate that admit you to the road.*

*Go right, then right again at the junction, around the right hand side of the Sea View public house and right again at the next junction by the giant Glaxo pharmaceutical works.*

The works occupy the site of the former North Lonsdale Iron Works – hence the slag heaps on the seaward side of the last stretch of the walk. The ironworks ceased producing iron in 1938. The company, known as Glaxochem, is part of the multinational Glaxo group and the Ulverston plant is the group's largest single manufacturing unit and one of the largest antibiotic producing plants in the world.

Since 1948, and starting with penicillin, many thousands of tonnes of antibiotics have been manufactured for conversion into doses for prescriptions. Specific moulds are fermented and the antibiotic is then extracted from the fermentation broth by precipitating them out and they are further purified before being packaged in pre-sterilised containers. The plant products include penicillin, cephalosporin, griseofulvin (for ringworm treatment) and vitamin B12 (for combating pernicious anaemia).

*Follow the road until it comes to the Bay Horse public house, (known for its high standard catering), by Canal Foot. Public toilets are just over the canal bridge. People walking from west to east will find the guide's house just past the front of the Inn.*

*Go along the towpath track on the far side of the canal all the way to Canal Head, Ulverston.*

## Ulverston Canal

Ulverston was an eighteenth-century iron ore port where up to a hundred and fifty ships involved in the coastal trade were once based. The development of Liverpool saw many ships move there to gain trade. The opening of the canal, in 1796, resulted in an ore quay being built by the nearby Newlands mining company and trade from coastal loading sites like Conishead Bank decreased to nothing. However, the canal suffered from the vagaries of the shifting Leven channel which, by moving away from the west bank, could make passage by the larger ships impossible. The mile and a half canal, one of only three built in Cumbria, could take ships of up to 400 tons to Ulverston. The canal made Ulverston an important sea port until the waterway was eclipsed by the railway in

the mid-nineteenth century, as well as suffering from the problem of the channel silting up. In 1798 it handled 94 ships with a tonnage of 4,700 tons whilst, at its peak in 1846, 946 ships of 61,000 tons used the canal. Iron ore, pig iron, bar iron, Kirkby Moor slate, limestone and grain were shipped out and Wigan coal was shipped in.

Until 1878, Ulverston was a shipbuilding town, most ships being built, after the canal opening, at Canal Head and Canal Foot. The town around this time was primarily a market town, its charter being granted in 1280, but it had textile mills for making cottons, linens, checks, sail canvas, woollen yarn and manufactured hats and ropes. In the early nineteenth century it was the biggest centre of population in the area.

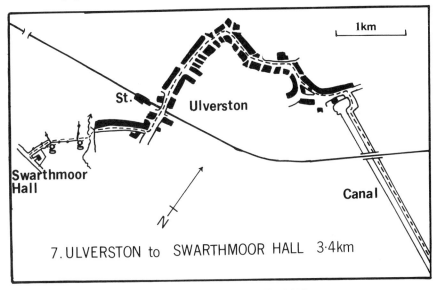

SKETCH MAP 7 and SD 17/27

# An Ulverston Town Trail

*Emerging on the main road from Canal Head go left, cross and follow the curve of Sunderland Terrace and its continuation into Hart Street and then Fountain Street to turn left into King Street and emerge at the market square.*

The dominant 'lighthouse' on the Hoad is a memorial to the famous son of Ulverston, Sir John Barrow, who held a high position in the admiralty. Barrow gave his name to several features on the North West Passage to the Pacific – an enterprise in which he played a leading role. He was also a founder of the Royal Geographical Society which, with Trinity House, funded the memorial. The lighthouse design, based on the Edison light, was used because Trinity House gave their donation provided the design was such and the lighthouse could be lit.

Other famous sons of Ulverston include Lord Birkett and Stan Laurel, to whom Ulverston hosts a museum which you pass near on this part of the route.

Sunderland Terrace was named after the Sunderland family and Col T. Sunderland is remembered as having cut the first sod of the canal. The long curving row of tall houses was built just before 1800, when they commanded a full length view of the canal and the estuary. The view was curtailed when the railway arrived in 1857 and the 'six bridges' were built. It is reputed that at one time each house was occupied by a mariner or person connected with the sea-faring trade.

The Lower School, or that portion of it now visible, is the most imposing building in Hart Street. Architecturally late Victorian in style, it was built in the early years of the present century as the Higher Grade and Technical School. A little further along on the left stands Hartley's Brewery which dates from some 150 years before the school and is still going strong under it ownership by Robinson's of Stockport. Hartley's very fine ales can be sampled at many Cistercian Wayside inns!

Fountain Street is narrower and older than Hart Street. The fine Georgian town house of the Mackereth family, and once the Liberal Club, is now a warehouse and semi-derelict, although there are now plans to renovate it. The Renaissance Theatre Company have their offices close by, in low two-storey premises of 17th-century origin.

As the junction of Soutergate and King Street is approached, the Kings Arms pub is directly ahead. Decorated with much fancy plasterwork, the present building of 1897 is a replacement of an older and humbler hostelry. The Kings Arms was once nicknamed 'The Klondike' because the landlord had made his fortune gold mining before returning to Ulverston. He was reputed to have displayed a gold nugget on the bar to commemorate his good fortune.

Now in the main shopping streets, there is still some 'olde worlde' atmosphere in the form of the Rose and Crown and Salmon's Café (with three datestones from three different centuries) and surely the only café in Britain which closes for lunch! Then there is James Atkinson's bookshop, established a century ago, and Peter Heal's shoe shop which occupies a former flour mill and warehouse.

The compact central area of the town, with winding streets – some still cobbled – lanes and ginnels, contains much of interest. Many stone buildings around the centre are late 17th-century. The War Memorial stands on the site of an earlier iron cross and the nearby buildings are mostly 18th-century. This is the hub of the town and especially of its market. The market is still held weekly on Thursdays and Saturdays after a charter was granted in 1280.

*Continue from King Street along the 'Royal Way' along Queen Street, cross the A590 at the traffic lights and then continue up Prince's Street to cross the railway bridge by the station.*

Queen Street contains several dignified buildings including former town houses of the Georgian period. The Globe Inn and the Kings Head were built much earlier and still retain their period interiors. Ulverston's Town Hall stands between Theatre Street and Benson Street. The area around the traffic lights was once known as Town End but the name is far from appropriate now.

The steeple of the former Holy Trinity Church dominates the skyline as County Road is crossed into Princes Street. The church, completed around 1835, has recently been converted into an indoor sports club. Several more town houses line the interesting street on the way to the railway station.

Ulverston Station, actually the town's third, was built in 1874 for the Furness Railway Company and was designed by the regional architects Paley and Austin, normally remembered for their church designs. The platform awnings are unusually fine but the majority of the station buildings have been sacrificed to become a nightclub. It has lost over half its wrought iron and glass canopies, its signal box and its refreshment rooms. However, it is still possible to feel the Victorian atmosphere through the remaining façade and awnings. Two original Furness Railway seats remain in the booking office, with their cast iron ends displaying the famous squirrel design.

Stage Five

# Ulverston – Great Urswick – Little Urswick – Dalton
*9.5 Kilometres (6 miles)*

SKETCH MAP 7 and SD 17/27    (see page 25)

*From Ulverston railway station continue along Springfield Road and, just after The Drive, on the right is a footpath sign on the nearside of the school. Go through the kissing gate and follow the enclosed path along and then down left to a bridge over the beck. The path then crosses the field to a gate and kissing gate through which an enclosed track leads, via a further kissing gate to a road with Swarthmoor Hall on your left.*

## Swarthmoor Hall

Swarthmoor Hall was the sixteenth-century home of Judge Fell, but is better known for its associations with the early Quaker movement and with George Fox in particular. The hall has been restored – Judge Fell's room still has a seventeenth-century fireplace, oak panelling and floors and an unusual oak newel staircase. The local meeting house (1688) with its burial ground is not far away.

Fox was a dynamic preacher, believing that wherever Christians gathered together was itself a place of worship and that paid clergy were an anathema. Fox was not well received in Ulverston – being beaten several times – but Judge Fell, although not himself a follower of the Quakers, welcomed him at Swarthmoor. Waugh tells the story that Fox was dragged from Swarthmoor Hall one night and kept in Ulverston under the guard of fifteen men, some of whom were perched in the fireplace, in case he should fly up the chimney! He was then taken to Lancaster Castle where he remained in prison for some time. Some years after Judge Fell died, Fox married his widow Margaret who was a convert to Quakerism. Because of his travels and sojourns in prison, however, Fox did not spend a lot of time at Swarthmoor.

Margaret Fell appears to have been a remarkable person in her own right. Not only did she become a Quaker, but she also convinced her judge husband to allow her persecuted Quaker friends to be welcome at Swarthmoor whenever they required. She sought royal intervention when some Quakers were imprisoned, she visited Friends who were in prison while still remaining a friend of King Charles II.

Set in beautiful grounds, Swarthmoor Hall is a fine building. Particularly lovely is its great bay window which goes up all three storeys, whilst the interior reflects the quintessence of Quakerism, peace and serenity. The long barn and brewhouse were lost through dilapidation but the house itself has been restored as nearly as possible to capture the atmosphere of Fell's and Fox's days. The large front door opens into the flagged passage that was once part of the Great Hall. Most of the contents of the still imposing Great Hall are not, alas, the originals. A newel staircase, which is original, gives access to the upper floors – there is only one other staircase like this in the country. Judge Fell's master bedroom and that of Margaret are fitted with suitable period pieces.

The hall is well worth visiting and should be included in your itinerary. It is open on Mondays, Tuesdays, Wednesdays and Saturdays from mid-March to mid-October from 10-12 and 2-5. At other times of the year and on Thursdays and Sundays visits by appointment can be made (see the section on useful addresses at the end of the book).

*With the hall to your rear go left along the road and right at the first junction unless you are to visit the Quaker Meeting House.*

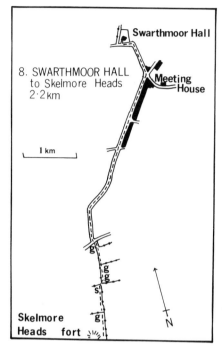

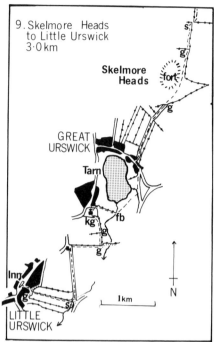

SKETCH MAP 8 and SD 17/27          SKETCH MAP 9 and SD 17/27

# Swarthmoor Meeting House

At the first junction Meeting House Lane lies opposite. Just a short way down this lane is the Quaker Meeting House built in 1688. On your way you pass number 4, Rakehead Cottages, where the key to visit the Meeting House can be obtained.

In 1691 George Fox purchased this property, then a small cottage and barn called Petty's, for £72. He wanted it to be used as a Quaker Meeting House as Swarthmoor could not, in those times, be expected to continue to provide facilities for worship. A large chair, owned by Fox, is still present. It was the first Meeting House built for the movement.

   The burial ground came into use about 1710 and, in spring, is covered in daffodils. The accommodation at the end of the building was originally used for worshippers' horses. Worship takes place at 10.45 each Sunday. Return to the road junction.

*Follow the road from its crossroads along until you meet a T junction. Leave the road by the middle of three gates facing you to re-enter the fields via the short enclosed track. Follow the right hand wall through two fields to a gate by the far right hand corner. Go through the gate and cross the short opening to a gap stile in the stone wall corner immediately opposite. Through the stile go left along the left hand wall, through the gate across your way and continue to follow the left hand wall until it bends away from you.*

## Skelmore Heads

The elongated tumulus hillfort earthworks on your right is called Skelmore Heads; the site was the subject of excavations in 1957 and 1959, without any great success. The hilltop site appears to have been used by Neolithic settlers but suggestions of occupation during Iron Age and Roman times are possibly accurate – the fort itself is said to be of Iron Age date. Some stone axes and pieces of bronze have been found on the site and are in Barrow museum. There is little apart from the view to be seen by ascending the hillock.

From the path you can also see to the south east the rough ground of Birkrigg Common, where there are remains of Bronze and Iron Age settlements including a double stone circle. A change in ancient pollen levels from nearby mosses suggests that the common was created as a shared pasture in the woodland clearances of the Middle Bronze Age.

There is also, on Skelmore Heads, the remains of a small mine shaft and buildings on your right as you pass by.

SKETCH MAP 9 and SD 17/27

*After the wall has bent away left continue along the foot of the stony ramparts of the hillfort and rejoin a wall from your left that funnels you to a gate. Go through the gate and follow the enclosed track all the way along and down to the road until the village of Great Urswick, with its tarn, enters your view.*

# Great Urswick

The field boundaries on this section of the walk are very straight and largely parallel to our enclosed track; these more recent boundaries disguise the open field which was created around 400AD. The walls and hedges will represent the strips of the open field, possibly, according to one theory, dating from the time of Anglian settlement in the seventh century, complete with their street of farmhouses along the northern side of the tarn and now called Great Urswick. However, the pollen evidence, coupled with the fact that the Anglo-Saxons and Norse people were mainly pastoral farmers in this region, suggests that there may have been woodland recolonisation here before the field was eventually recleared for arable farming as late as the twelfth and thirteenth centuries due to growing population pressures and the developing economy of Furness Abbey. This gives rise to the possibility that the open field was the product of the late Roman Iron Age settlers of Skelmore Heads laying out the field for their use before other settlers came to the tarnside site.

John Parker tells the tale that the tarn has an odd legend about a sunken village. A priest, so the story goes, tired of the constant complaints about the lack of water for the village cattle (nothing unusual in such limestone country) and of the suggestion that he was worthless for doing nothing about it, turned his back on the village and induced an earthquake which destroyed the settlement and replaced it with a tarn. Although John admits that the story is "ridiculous" he also asks why the church is so far from the present village? The tarn was core sampled in 1960 when a 6 metre core was taken from the southern edge in order to examine the ancient layers of tree pollen and thus provide a history of the woods and agriculture back through several thousand years.

SKETCH MAP 9 and SD 17/27

*Turn left along the road, go right at the junction and then go down to the side of Urswick Tarn. Continue along to a stile and in the tarnside field go along to the gate and then continue to cross the beck from the tarn by a footbridge. In the next field follow the right hand boundary up to the rear of St. Mary and St. Michael's church.*

# Urswick Church

The church of St Mary and St Michael is full of excellent wood carvings, partially due to the Chipping Camden Guild. The church replaced a Norman building but there are fragments of an earlier, ninth-century Anglo-Saxon cross with Runic inscriptions which read "this cross Tunwini erected in memory of Thorhtred, a monument to his lord. Pray for the soul". Another, later, cross shaft reflects the Viking settlement. The church has Cistercian connections dating back to before Furness was established. Outside, on the porch, can be seen the scratches made when arrows were sharpened during practices after services, and the remains of a mass dial and chain links left from the barrier erected to keep the vicar's cow from sleeping in the porch. The porch was used for sleeping when people stayed under its shelter for two nights after a burial in order to prevent grave robbers from doing their dirty work.

Inside there is a three storey pulpit with a sounding board, stained glass windows with fragments from Furness Abbey (in the lancet window) as well as the coats of arms of local families. There is also a hagioscope.

The painting of the last supper is by a local artist James Cranke (1707-1781) who was a tutor of the famous Kendal artist Romney (see the description of Dalton Church later).

The church still maintains a rushbearing ceremony, dating from when local people perpetuated the tradition of placing rushes on the earthen floor, partly as a practical step and partly as a symbolic mark of renewal. This celebration is held in September. The siting of the church between Great and Little Urswick suggests that both villages grew up near open fields fashioned in Roman times and that both villages were settled more or less simultaneously by Anglian farmers, who chose a site convenient to both places in which to build a church. The cross fragment adds some additional evidence to the pollen and field records for the history of the area.

Nearby, but not on our route, lies the remains of a Neolithic or early Bronze Age burial chamber set in a rough pasture, with many limestone boulders making it appear more like a natural feature.

SKETCH MAP 9 and SD 17/27

*To continue, follow the path at the rear, by the south east corner, of the church and parallel to the wall which was on your left when you entered the churchyard. This leads to a kissing gate and into a field. When you have gone through the gate bear slightly left and a swing gate will be found in the far left hand corner of this field. Go through, and along the left hand hedge to the next red, swing gate. Go through, turn right and follow the hedge bank on your right up to the village recreation hall by the road. Go left along the enclosed bridlepath at the rear of the hall.*

This section of the walk also passes through fields whose long narrow shapes and straight walls and hedges reflect the strips of another former open field on the east side of Little Urswick. Again, as below Skelmore Heads, the history of the landscape is still open to a range of interpretations, awaiting more archaeological investigation and a greater understanding of the period before yielding up the secrets of its past.

*Just before the bridlepath ends at the road, go right through a red kissing gate on the near side of the bridge. In the field follow the right hand hedge bank up towards Little Urswick. Two swing gates on the right of the red field gates lead you through to the farm yard. Go across the first track and then continue up the yard to reach the village green opposite the school near the Swan Inn where refreshments can be obtained.*

SKETCH MAP 10 and SD 17/27

*To continue go between the permanent and temporary school buildings, pass over a couple of stiles and cross a short enclosure to a swing gate. In the next field, with much scrub, go parallel to the right hand boundary, pass the end of*

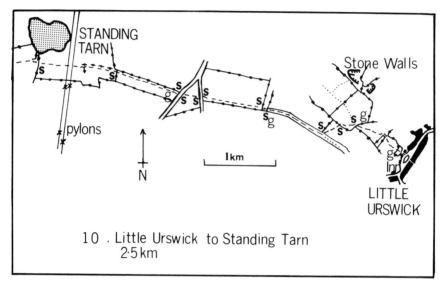

SKETCH MAP 10 and SD 17/27

*the wire fenced enclosure on your left, and then go uphill to a gap stile by a gate in the wall facing you where it meets an old hedge bank to your left. Go through the stile and strike half left to cut the field corner and reach a further gap stile through which you pass.*

Nearby, and easily reached by a path from this side of the gap stile by the gate, is one of the most impressive fragments of pre-history in north-west England and which goes under the prosaic name of Stone Walls.

These are two enclosed ramparts of stone and earth, one oval shaped, one rectangular, the former having the foundations of a large hut. Flint scrapers and parts of granite querns along with animal bones and a thin, engraved strip of bronze (dated by its pattern to the 1st or 2nd century B.C.) have been found. This was probably a single farmstead occupied for a couple of centuries before Roman times and was mainly used for stock rearing – the walls giving protection against wolves. There was possibly an arable field adjacent to the farm to cater for the occupant's grain needs. The site is difficult to interpret unless you have details (see Barnes, F., or Millward and Robinson).

*Over this stile cross the field to a stile in the hedge facing you by the far right hand corner. Through this stile you enter a lane which you follow up to your right until it ends with a stile and gate. Go over this stile, cross the short side of the field to the stone gap stile and then follow the long left hand hedge bank along and down.*

*At the bottom of the field a further gap stile some 10m to the right of the overhead wire post will give you access to a narrow road with a further stile and gate directly across the lane. Use this stile to gain access to the next field and cross to a further stile – with wooden and stone uprights – to give access to the next lane.*

*Again cross the road to a metal gate with a narrow gap stile on its right. This gives access to a long, narrow field through which you pass by the right hand boundary. At the far end, a stile in the corner gives access to a large field. Continue in the same direction as before to contour across the field, passing two thorns and one tree and then the remains of an old field boundary corner by two small thorns. Pass under the overhead power cables with Standing Tarn down to your right. Leave the field by descending slightly to a stile in the boundary that rises from the tarn – the stile is immediately above the line of trees.*

On the left are the red spoil tips of an old iron ore mine. The area around Dalton, Lindal and Askam are littered with these reminders of what was once the major industry in this part of Furness. Some, like Park Mine, were huge, others much smaller. There is little left to interpret this industry and most books on the industry, like that by Fell, are out of print. There is great scope for someone to bring research in this area up to date and for some interpretive facilities on the mines and miners.

SKETCH MAP 11 and SD 17/27 (see page 36)

*Climb the rise in the next field by going straight ahead and then go to a stile by a gate in the far right hand corner of the field. Over the stile go right on the track but climb the stile on the left just after the blue gate. In the field follow the right hand boundary along and down, with views of Dalton ahead, to a further stile by a gate. Over the stile go left and down to a track by some houses. Follow the access track down and under the railway and then continue along to the main road. Go left along the main road to the centre of Dalton at Tudor Square.*

Stage Six

# Dalton To Furness Abbey
*3 Kilometres (2 miles)*

SKETCH MAP 11 and SD 17/27

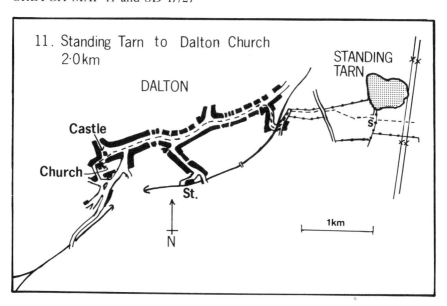

11. Standing Tarn to Dalton Church
2·0 km

STANDING TARN

DALTON

Castle

Church

St.

N

1km

*From Tudor Square go towards Barrow down Market Street and at the junction, where the road to Barrow goes left, continue up to the castle.*

## Dalton Town Trail

Tudor Square has a neo-Tudor fronted inn and some 18th-century low two-storey cottages with more modern shop fronts.

Going westwards down Market Street some of the 19th-century terraced housing can be seen. Many were built to house the iron-ore miners who worked here, especially between 1860 and 1914 when the area's mines were prosperous. Part way along you enter Dalton Conservation Area. Of interest amid the buildings are the façades of 97/99 Market Street; 51 Market Street with its unique cast iron shop frontage; Courts 5 and 6; and Court 3 (between 1 and 3 Market Street).

The Market Place has several interesting buildings – 19 is said to be a former pub where John Wesley preached; 13-19 all have stepped roofs; 5A dates from 1683 and is little altered; whilst the Red Lion Inn (18th-century) has what used to be a carriage entry.

1 to 3 Skelgate and the Vicarage on the west side of the square, are probably Georgian houses but it is the fountain and the castle which command attention. The cast iron drinking fountain has a counterpart in Askam. The fluted columns support a dome openwork roof, with the fountain on a pedestal beneath the canopy. It probably dates from 1897.

Nearby are the Market Cross and slabs of stone used as fish drying slabs (mid 19th-century). The Court Leet for the Manors of Plain Furness were held bi-annually under the cross in the square, during which the rents of tenants in the manor were collected. This feudal arrangement continued until the passing of the 1922 Law of Property Act – the last session being 24th October 1923.

The fourteenth-century Pele tower, Dalton Castle, was originally constructed in around 1330-1336 to provide a place of refuge for the monks of Furness Abbey against the Scottish raiders. It has been greatly altered internally over the centuries but retains most of its original external features.

The area of the castle and church is believed to be the original hilltop site of the 'Dale Town' and both Stone and Bronze Age artefacts have been discovered in the vicinity. Dalton probably became the first market town in the area when the monks of Furness began holding fairs and markets in the thirteenth century. The decline of Dalton coincided roughly with the dissolution of Furness Abbey and the growing importance of Greenodd and Ulverston as ports.

Visiting arrangements are displayed on the door of the castle, which is in National Trust ownership. The castle contains a small museum. Go down the left hand side of the castle and you will come to the Church of St Mary. It was designed by Paley and Austin and Pevsner calls it one of their "most spectacular". It is built of sandstone (1885) with a five-sided, south-facing porch and elaborate geometrical fenestration. Its main claim to fame is the gravestone of the famous artist Romney (1706-1802).

*After visiting this, continue down the lane passing the church to the bottom of the hill. Here there is the circular rubble wall of the old pound. Turn right just before the main road and follow the track to the last houses and a gate.*

SKETCH MAP 12 and SD 17/27

*Through the gate continue along the track, once fully enclosed, with the beck below on your left. Continue under the railway bridge and cross the field to an interesting old packhorse bridge.*

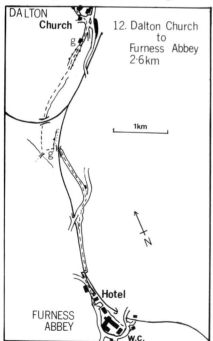

12. Dalton Church to Furness Abbey 2·6 km

1km

N

The bridge appears to be mid 15th-century in date and connected with the Abbey. It does not appear to have been researched.

*Do NOT cross but turn left and cross the field to a small gate and track that takes you under a further railway bridge and along a track past a house, to the main road.*
*    Cross the road directly to a further path that leads through a wood, alongside the railway, going under a bridge and continuing with the railway on your left to the road, pub and gatehouse museum of Furness Abbey.*

Alongside the Vale of Deadly Nightshade, (once the dale of Beckansgill) where, just over the railway, lies Abbotswood, an area of Local Natural History Interest with its nature trail, which is well worth following. The Abbotswood grounds were once part of the now demolished house of Sir James Ramsden of Furness Railway fame.

# Furness Abbey

### History of the Abbey

Stephen Count of Blois, who later became King of England (1135-1154), established an Abbey at Tulketh in Preston in 1123. It was a Savignac house but in 1127 the monks moved north to the more remote and suitable Furness site; indeed, the name Furness has been translated as 'obscure'. Twenty years later the order was absorbed by the Cistercians.

The site was remote, a complaint sometimes heard about modern day Barrow, and to reach the Abbey the tidal sands of Morecambe Bay and the Leven had to be crossed. This treacherous route had claimed the lives of over 140 people and so eventually the Abbeys provided salaried guides to the sands crossings. The site of the Abbey was waste or marshy ground and the buildings foundations are laid on large pieces of oak placed in the soft ground. However, the district had all the natural resources that the monks could wish for.

Furness Abbey received rich endowments of land, including some in Yorkshire and Ireland. In addition to the local agriculture, wool, iron (made from the local ores) and charcoal making made substantial contributions to the Abbey's wealth. Indeed the iron industry development, along with the wool trade, proved to be the foundation of the Abbey's economic success. The Furness *Coucher Book* provides historians with their earliest printed records of the iron industry in Furness. Some of the output from the Abbey's bloomery went to tenants for their agricultural implements.

There were some disadvantages for the monks, mainly that the site lay on the route of the Scottish invaders and thus suffered from their raids. In fact the Scottish border was far from fixed when the Abbey was established – at one time it followed the adjacent Duddon estuary.

The suppression of the Abbey came early in the dissolution (1537) and this was partially due to some Furness monks taking part in the Northern Rebellion against the closure of the monasteries known as the Pilgrimage of Grace.

Two other historical events are worth noting. In 1487 Lambert Simnel landed his army nearby on his way to attempt to depose King Henry VII. Simnel left the Abbey untouched and also failed miserably in his intention.

The other incident, dating perhaps from the twelfth century, involved an ex-monk of Furness called Wimund who had turned pirate and used this knowlesge of the gathering wealth of the Abbey to good effect. He wrought havoc both in Scotland and against the Abbey's possessions before being ambushed and blinded. Earlier he had been made Bishop of the Isle of Man.

Henry VIII, on dissolution, granted the abbey lands to his chief minister Thomas Cromwell. In 1756 they were transferred to the local landowning family the Cavendishes of Holker Hall. The monastery passed back to government hands in 1923. It is now in the hands of English Heritage who are exercising much thought and expending much money to ensure the Abbey's future as one of its northern gems.

# The Cistercians

The Cistercian order was founded in 1098 at Citeaux, in Burgundy, by monks who wanted to return to the simplicity and austerity of life as it had been in the early days of the Benedictine order. They wore white habits with black aprons and soon became known as the 'White Monks'. The principles on which the order was founded included dwelling in isolation and thus being removed from worldly distraction, to attain peace and discipline, for prayers, study of the scriptures and meditation.

At the time of the foundation of the Abbey at Furness the site was wild, though the dale had once been the home of Norse settlers. Soon after the foundation the principles of the order seemed to take a back pew as the acquisition of wealth in the form of lands and property as well as from trade and industry became greater priorities.

No doubt the building costs of the Abbey were a constant drain on funds, as were the costs of land reclamation and economic development, thus turning the monks into successful entrepreneurs. The extensive commercialisation and the generous interest of patrons ensured that by the time of dissolution only Fountains Abbey was a richer Cistercian house.

# Tour of the Abbey

The Abbey is under the care of English Heritage and entry, upon payment, is made by the gatehouse and museum. Like all Cistercian houses it is dedicated to St. Mary the Virgin and it is the church that best gives an impression of the scale of the Abbey buildings. The walls of the tower, transepts and chancel retain their full height, whilst the nave walls only hint at their former grandeur.

On your way to the Cemetery Gate and church from the museum you pass the foundations of the Guest House and adjacent is a stone threshold inscribed for a game of nine mens morris.

The church was 100 metres long and contains some of the earliest building work. It was substantially complete by the end of the twelfth century. The belfry tower was added around 1500 – complete with the interesting gargoyles that still peer down from the outer face. There is no west door because of the tightness of the site – the whole building is sandwiched in a narrow vale. This also explains why the building lies north east-south west rather than on the normal east-west axis. The nave has ten bays but a stone screen was built across during the thirteenth century in order to assign part of the church for the lay brethren. The piers, of which only foundations remain, were alternately clustered and circular.

The monks tried to rebuild the low belfry in the crossing during the fifteenth century in a more elaborate style but the foundations proved inadequate and so the tower was finally built at the western end. The transept arches still remain, reflecting Cistercian simplicity of style. Repair work revealed that the monks reinforced their foundations by laying down oak tree trunks. Outside the north transept door is a wall that separated the monks cemetery from the outer court. Several tombstones remain unmoved.

The chancel or presbytery was a fifteenth-century addition – perhaps the tower on the crossing that collapsed destroyed the original. The building contained some stained glass windows made by Sir John Petty of York. The base

of the high altar remains and on the south wall are the sedilia and piscina. The former was seating for the officiating clergy and has tall, canopied heads with Tudor flower cresting that earns it the description of "the most magnificent in the country".

The south transept housed the night stairs to the dormitory. On the left of the cloisters are two barrel vaulted chambers which served as book cupboards. Between these two is a vaulted vestibule which led to the chapter house. Here the monks would gather daily for monastic business and where a chapter of the monastic rule book was read. This is thirteenth-century work described as having "graceful simplicity typical of the best work of the period".

Adjacent is a small parlour where the monks could talk without breaking the silence of the cloister. Just south is the passage to the dorter. This dormitory, at 57 metres long, is thought to be the largest of any in an English monastery. It must have been a cold, damp, draughty place to sleep. Outside, at the rear, and over the stream was the reredorter (latrines) and a guest house. Next to the dorter and the cloisters once stood a warming house where the brethern no doubt congregated during the cooler months.

Over the western side of the cloisters are the foundations of the octagonal kitchen and refectory of the lay brethern (and their dormitory would have been above). South of these buildings lies the infirmary (early fourteenth-century) with its own chapel and kitchen still standing. This large hall with triangular headed windows also had a fireplace. Across the beck are the ruins of the Abbot's house which probably stands on the site of an earlier infirmary. The whole monastic precinct was enclosed by a wall, of which sections can still be seen, particularly to the south-east of the site.

# Wordsworth and Furness Abbey

William Wordsworth visited the abbey whilst a pupil at Hawkshead Grammar School. He recalls the visit in his Prelude (Book ii):

> ". . . a Structure famed
> Beyond its neighbourhood, the antique walls
> Of that large Abbey which within the Vale
> Of Nightshade, to St Mary's honour built,
> Stands yet, a mouldering Pile, with fractured Arch,
> Belfry, and Images, and living Trees,
> A holy Scene !"

Wordsworth returned around 1840 and wrote the first of two poems entitled 'Furness Abbey'. In the first he describes the work of the elements in slowly demolishing the Abbey and blames the Cavendish family for its neglect of the site.

Several years later, in 1845, he revisited the Abbey whilst the railway line was being built adjacent to the site. The sight of the navvies spending their lunch break amongst the ruins also moved him to a second poem 'At Furness Abbey'. He uses the poem to criticise the builders of the railway as despoilers but praises the reverence and wonder of the navvies at the Abbey's construction.

Wordsworth had also compiled his Ecclesiastical Sonnets and two of these are entitled 'Cistercian Monastery'. Sonnet Three begins with a translation of the Latin quotation found at all Cistercian houses:

"Here Man more purely lives, less oft doth fall,
More promptly rises, walks with stricter heed,
More safely rests, dies happier, is freed
Earlier from cleansing fires, and gains withal
A brighter crown".

What better than to read all these poems as you pause amongst the ruins?

## OPENING TIMES

The Abbey is open from 15th March to 15th October at the following times:

Weekdays 09.30 to 18.30, Sundays 14.00 to 18.30.

For the remainder of the year the times are:

Weekdays 09.30 to 13.00, Sundays 14.00 to 16.00.

44

Stage Seven

# Furness Abbey To Roa Island And Piel Island
## 11 Kilometres (7 miles)

SKETCH MAP 13 and SD 17/27.

*After your visit to the Abbey follow the road alongside the Abbey until you pass the car park and toilets on your right.*

The football field by the car park is the site of the Abbey's Fish Tanks and above the bank lies part of the Abbey wall.

*After the house a footpath leaves the right hand side of the road (signed Parkhouse Road) to cross the railway by a level crossing as the railway emerges*

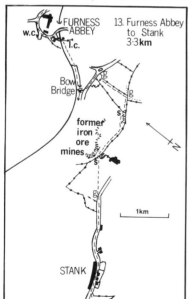

*from a short tunnel. Go right in the field and follow alongside the railway to reach Bow Bridge crossing a stream by a bridge on the way.*

The bridge is medieval and was associated with a corn mill from the Abbey.

*Cross the bridge and go to the road and then left to the road junction. On your right is a battered iron kissing gate which gives you access to the fields. Climb half right to a bend in the old field boundary, go through a gap and then go uphill with the boundary by your left. Near the top, in the boundary facing you, is a swing gate.*
*Do not pass through this gate but turn right with this boundary now on your left to reach a stile. Cross and continue near the left hand boundary as you climb towards the highest part of the knoll ahead.*

The knoll gives superb views of Barrow and the Furness peninsula and, on a clear day, of the Lakeland Fells. This area is pitted with the remains of iron ore mines.

There was little mining in the manor of Furness in the late seventeenth century but coal was found in a mine at Stank in 1696 when the mine had been opened without the permission of the Lord of the Manor. It was looking for coal in this mine, in later years, that led to the accidental discovery of the Stank ore deposit.

*When the steep drop on the right becomes fenced look for a wooden stile in the boundary on your left. Cross this into the corner of the field with a wooded depression on your left. Cross the field to your right by following the overhead wires (with Morecambe Bay ahead) to reach a swing gate by a wooden fence in the boundary on your left, just above a line of hawthorns that marked an old field boundary.*

*Go right, down the road, to the hamlet of Stank.*

SKETCH MAP 14 and SD 17/27 and 16/26.

*Continue through the hamlet to pass the last building on the left, go along the roadside wall and then, on the left, through a stile by a gate and footpath sign (Leece) in the hedge.*

*In the field go up the slope on the left aiming towards the twin pylons to a stile by two stone gate posts where the hedge crosses the small beck. Through the*

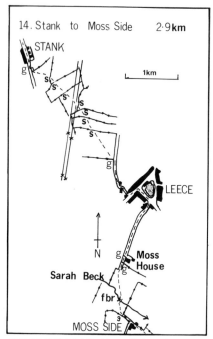

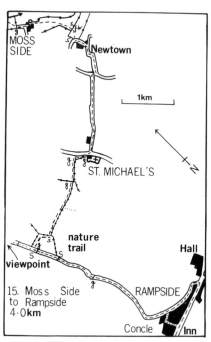

SKETCH MAP 14 & SD 17/27, 16/26          SKETCH MAP 15 & SD 16/26

*stile go half right to pass through another narrow gap stile above a gate. Cross
the next field, aiming right of the pylons, to cross the next stile in the hedge
facing you.*

*Pass under the overhead wires to the right of the pylon to a further stile above
a boulder in the hedge on the banking. Over this go half right to a stile in the
right hand hedge and then cross to continue the slight climb to cross a stile in
the hedge facing you by aiming to the topmost overhead wire pole. In this next
field go half left to climb the field to a gate in the furthermost corner under the
overhead wires. Through the gate go right and down the enclosed track to the
road at Leece.*

*Turn left on the road and then first right with the village duck pond on your
left. Turn right at the cross roads by the end of the village green and climb the
metalled access road over the hillock and down to Moss House Farm. Keep to
the right of the house to pass through a stile by the gate, go down the enclosed
green track, pass through a further gate and continue down into the bottom
field.*

*In the field go half left, aiming right of the next farm, to reach a footbridge
across Sarah Beck. Over the bridge go half left across the field to a gate and
track to Moss Side Farm.*

*SKETCH MAP 15 and SD 16/26.*

*Keep to the left of the first building, pass through the gated yard and leave by a gap between the slurry tank and shippon. Go ahead through the gate facing you and then continue along the left hand boundary. When this bends off left continue in the same direction to skirt the right hand hillock and then meet a hedge coming down from the right. Go along the right hand hedge to the field corner where a small footbridge gives access to the last field before a white painted house. In this last field aim to the right of the house to reach a further stile and an enclosed lane.*

*Go left on the lane and continue past the house when it becomes metalled. Keep right at the bungalow, turn right and then first left on the narrow roads to eventually reach, after crossing the A5087, St Michael's Church, Rampside.*

# Rampside Church

Why the church should be so far from the village remains a mystery – possibly resolved by the possibility that a 'lost' village may once have been near this site. The church can be traced back to 1621 and we know that Rampside was the site of an Abbey Grange (farm) of around a hundred acres.

George Fox once spoke from the pulpit and 'converted' the incumbent, Thomas Lawson, to the Quaker faith. Lawson was also a noted botanist. One vicar ran a boarding school at Rampside. Rampside itself was the site of an abbey grange (farm) of around a hundred acres.

SKETCH MAP 15 and SD 16/26

*From the church go towards Barrow to a gate alongside the church with footpath and nature trail signs. Go through the gate, down the sloping path and through the next gate. In this next field go left to follow the fence, pass a gate and then climb besides the left hand hedge to a gate and stile across your way. Over this hurdle follow the left hand hedge and where it is met by a fence and stile cross and go half right to a gate in the far right hand corner of the field. Go through this gate to reach a path fenced on both sides.*

*If you go right and climb the short hill you will see the etched viewpoint overlooking Barrow, Walney Channel, Walney Island and the gas terminal. Go back to the stile.*

*Go left over the stile and follow the enclosed path over a further stile, through a gate and continue for some distance on what is now a track to reach the road at Rampside.*

*SKETCH MAP 16 and SD 16/26.* (over page)

*Turn right along the road and go past Concle Inn and along the causeway, built for the railway, to Roa Island.*

# Rampside

The seventeenth-century Rampside Hall farmhouse with its ridge display of 12 chimneys and, perhaps, the pub, are the only likely distractors in this area the planners "let go". The Hall lies a few metres to your left when you join the road.

In the sixteenth century there was a 133 acre wood at Rampside "over and above marshy ground, growing there 500 young plants 800 old scrude oaks and 50 dotered oaks serving for reparation of tenants houses & for piles in the breaches & weares in the Ilande of Wanoo". By 1649 the wood had disappeared; because no one was responsible for its maintenance, it had suffered from lack of proper management and coppicing, and had gradually withered away over the years.

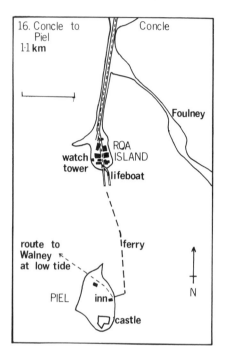

SKETCH MAP 16 and SD 16/26

# Roa Island

The island is now joined by causeway to the mainland and is indistinguishable from it. The railway company built this umbilical cord to carry their rails from the island's steamer pier from where tourists could dismbark, entrain and be taken around the Lakes on Furness Railway Company metals and lake steamer.

The causeway was built, along with the pier, by a John Abel Smith and the steamer service operated to Fleetwood. This action caused the railway company to build their port at Barrow rather than pay dues to Smith for this deep water harbour for sending out the iron ore. Smith described the causeway as connecting "Roa Island with Great Britain".

In 1852 the pier was damaged in a storm and the Furness Railway Company purchased Smith's interests for £15,000 and rebuilt the pier and causeway.

The lifeboat house sits proudly above the waters of Walney Channel a few paces away from one of Schneider's houses, Schneider was an iron ore dealer in the last century. From here you can also catch the small ferry boat to Piel Island.

# Piel Island

Piel Island boasts both a castle and a pub whose licensee is 'crowned' King of Piel. The island is a favourite port of call for sailing enthusiasts from the Lancashire coast as well as for Barrovians. If Piel was near a larger conurbation, the feeling of remoteness and much of the romance of the castle would be lost. We can be thankful that you can enjoy it in the relative tranquility of the place. Nonetheless, English Heritage are spending money on the castle which the previous owners neglected for too long.

Piel served as a harbour in early centuries. Baines in his *History of Lancashire* quotes from a report of the reign of Queen Elizabeth I, in which it is stated that "Between Mylford Haven in Wales and Carlisle . . . there is not one good haven for greate shyppes to londe or ryde in but one whiche is in the furthest part of Lancashire called Pylle of Fodder." Indeed in 1720 the local custom house was at Rampside, before transferring to Ulverston following changes in the pattern of iron ore shipments. The implication is that Piel served as a shipping harbour for the early iron ore industry in Low Furness.

The monks gained the land from Rampside, along with Piel, whose harbour became important to their commercial life. Although it was never completed, the castle was built by the monks of Furness Abbey in order to guard the entry to the channel from whence went their wealth of wool and iron. It also served as a base for their contraband running!

Henry IV questioned the monks' right to the castle when they apparently failed to maintain a proper garrison and they in turn feared the King might

appoint a Revenue Officer, which would have undermined their wool trade. The monks actually went as far as taking off the roof to make it uninhabitable but Henry's men did occupy the castle for some time, as well as taking Walney from the monks. The Abbot regained control and Barnes records that in the reign of

Henry VI the Flemish merchants were using Piel to avoid tax on the wool trade. Tenants of the crown in High Furness had to undertake to man the castle should there be a need to defend the realm.

Much remains intact of the sandstone fortification but the seaward side has lost some of its grandeur. However, one cannot help but feel that the collapsed walls ought to be repaired and the castle fully restored.

It was on Piel in 1487 that Lambert Simnel, pretender to the English throne, landed with about 8,000 men. After marching via Ulverston and the cross-bay routes, Simnel's army continued south until it was destroyed at Stoke-on-Trent. In the late sixteenth century, it appears that Piel was considered as a target for a bridgehead by the Spanish Armada. Later, in the eighteenth century, a revenue cutter (a tax man's boat for meeting ships with taxable commodities) was based on Piel.

From here, suitably refreshed, you could return to Roa but at low tide the drying sands may tempt you to walk the odd mile or so across to Walney Island by way of Sheep Island to Snab Point (see the next chapter). The sands you cross, which are also used by vehicles going to Piel, are part of a Site of Special Scientific Interest with a warden in attendance. This is an area of wintering wildfowl feeding and roosting – where species like shelduck, turnstone, oystercatcher, eider, teal, great crested grebe, dunlin and redshank can be spotted. We can see part of the area better from the route around Westfield Point.

# Foulney

Walking from Roa back to the original mainland at Rampside you will be aware of the more natural causeway linking Foulney Island. This shingle ridge links another SSSI which is famed for its bird life and flora. In this case terns are the speciality and, again, the site is wardened; access is discouraged during the breeding season.

Stage Eight

# To Barrow and on to Walney
### 7.5 Kilometres (4 miles)

There are two ways to reach Barrow. From Piel, at low tide, see Sketch Maps 19 and 20, walk to Snab Point on Walney and, after visiting the South End Nature Reserve, you can follow the road to Biggar village and then via Vickerstown to the bridge connecting the island to Barrow.

The alternative, which is favoured, is to walk from Roa Island back along the causeway towards Rampside. From Roa Island to Barrow you will be following the first stretch of the Cumbria Coastal Way, another medium-distance route which continues for one hundred miles around the coast and up to Carlisle.

SKETCH MAP 17 and SD 16/26.

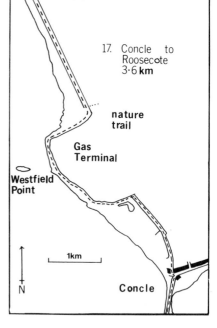

*Facing you at the end of the causeway, where the road bends right, is the house which was once the old Rampside station (the earthbank besides the footpath is all that remains of the old platform). Go to the right of the house and follow the enclosed track and in so doing traverse along the bed of the railway on what is part of the Westfield Nature Trail.*

SKETCH MAP 17 and SD 16/26

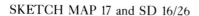

*When a gate bars your way go left down the enclosed path which is then followed around the headland of Westfield Point with the gas terminal to your right. In going round the point you have left the old railway track bed but this is rejoined on the far side of the terminal. The straight line of the old railway is then followed along to pass the former Roosecote Power Station.*

*former Roosecote Power Station.*

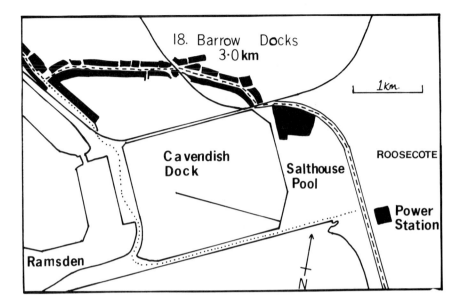

The terminal is where, in winter, British Gas brings natural gas ashore from the Morecambe Bay field, some 25 miles out to sea. British Gas have a leaflet available.

The spread of Roosecote Sands to your left, particularly around Westfield Point, gives ample opportunities for bird watchers to stand and observe the varied species. The rocks of Ridding Head stand out above the flow tide and thus make a favourite roosting place.

Above us and to the right, on the route between the Gas Terminal and the power station, are the Pulverised Fuel Ash (PFA) lagoons from the power station which, when full, were stabilised and then grassed over. Some steps up these provide a higher viewpoint of the sands and across to Walney. The power station used to burn an average of 2,500 tons of coal per week. Although closed by the CEGB there was a prospect of it becoming a private power station, supplying current to the National Grid.

At the power station it is possible, informally, to walk to the left around the seaward edge of Cavendish Dock, the largest of the four basins. This large basin of open water was never used by ships but was used as a cooling water system by the power station – to the delight of overwintering wildfowl.

*To reach the centre of Barrow either continue past the power station site and follow the track that leads under the railway and eventually reaches metalled roads. Go left to the town centre down the Strand. Or, if you have gone around*

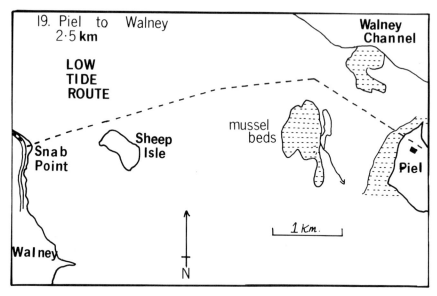

SKETCH MAP 19

*Cavendish Dock turn right at the end of the basin with Ramsden and Buccleuch Docks to your left and follow the track to Cavendish Road to emerge near the town centre and the Strand.*

# Walney Island

Walney Island is some 13 kilometres long and almost 2 kilometres wide in places. The southernmost land in the county of Cumbria, it was also a site occupied by early settlers after the last Ice Age – by Mesolithic hunter-fishermen.

Archaeological finds of flints used for barbs of harpoons and arrowtips, scrapers and knives for dealing with animals and their skins as well as for carving wood and bone, have been made. Some of the axes were made from pebbles taken from local boulder clay cliffs, whilst others came from the Neolithic traffic of Lakeland axe 'rough outs' some 3,000 years ago. Our current archaeological evidence suggests that in the three thousand years of prehistory, from Neolithic to Iron Age, the settlements in Low Furness were mainly around Urswick, Stainton and Walney.

The main axe factory site was at North End but remains of Mesolithic and Beaker peoples have been found elsewhere on the island. This industrial site was in use something like 5,000 years ago and involved trade with Ireland, as well as the more central Lake District.

The name Walney appears to have been derived from 'walled island', being descriptive of either the walls of stones pushed up the beaches by the sea or of walls built by early settlers. Another suggestion for the name uses a derivative of Hougenai or Haakon's island.

Furness Abbey had an influence on the island and its landscape through the three grange farms it held by the mid-thirteenth century. It also undertook some drainage work and a protective dyke, originally built under the auspices of the monks, can be seen north of Biggar.

Today much of the island is a downgraded landscape. Poorly maintained field boundaries, 'horseyculture', difficult farming conditions, over conspicuous caravan sites and rubbish tipping – both formal and otherwise – add to the problems.

Set against this you have the interest of the old smugglers' village of Biggar, where you can still find a close-knit community, two important nature reserves and the Vickerstown Conservation Area. For these attractions the island is well worth visiting.

## South Walney Reserve and Lighthouse

Here we are near to the South Walney Site of Special Scientific Interest and Nature Reserve. Once an area of mineral workings, it is now the most important and largest breeding site in Europe for Lesser Black Backed and Herring Gulls. It is the most southerly point in Cumbria. The shingle beach flora and the beach erosional and deposition features add further interest to site visitors. The site is permanently wardened by Cumbria Trust for Nature Conservation who run the reserve. Ring plovers and roseate terns also breed here whilst the eider is here at its southernmost breeding place in Britain. There are many interesting plants as well.

Admission is by permit only and this can be obtained at the warden's house by the reserve, apart from Mondays (Bank Holidays excepted). May and June are the best times to visit.

The Trinity House lighthouse on South End Haws was built for £1,000 in 1799 and serves as a guide to shipping from Morecambe Bay by way of Walney to Barrow docks. It is maintained by the service's only female lighthouse keeper. This listed building is not open to the public.

## Biggar

The hamlet of Biggar is a compact, introspective looking settlement which retains some character. Local building materials – cobbled walls or roughcast facing and slate roofs, together with the layout of the hamlet itself – add to the feeling of a haven of shelter and, perhaps, of secrecy and smuggling. Inside the hamlet change is taking place; old agricultural barns are becoming homes and the sense of history and character are being eroded. However, wander around the small village with particular attention to Town End Farm, New Inn, Manor Farmhouse, Hill Farm, Piel View Farm and the Queens Arms.

Just outside Biggar is Biggar Dyke. This embankment was constructed by the monks of Furness Abbey to protect their adjacent fields from the tides. After the Dissolution the tenants were allowed reduced rents in recognition of their responsibilities for maintaining the dyke. However, neglect set in and there are court records of tenants being fined for not providing their share of labour for the task.

# Walney North End

The other area of importance for natural history is the north tip of the island – the North End Site of Special Scientific Interest. It lies beyond the airfield and a permit should be obtained to visit the area, which includes many plants of interest and the rare natterjack toad.

Just off North End is Scarth Hole, a permanent stretch of water which holds some interesting marine life, including an Australian barnacle that reached here on the bottom of World War II convoy ships.

# Vickerstown

Just west of the bridge and promenade

SKETCH MAP 20

20. Walney

1 Sheep Island
2 Snab Point
3 Biggar
4 Dyke
5 Vickerstown
6 Jubilee Bridge
7 Barrow Island
8 Cavendish &
9 Ramsden
Docks

is Vickerstown, declared a Conservation Area in 1987. This settlement was conceived as a private housing venture by the Isle of Walney Estate Company as part of the overall development of the island as a resort during the mid-nineteenth century and in conjunction with a substantial expansion of the shipbuilding facilities across the channel – again called Vickers or, more correctly, VSEL.

The company found itself in financial difficulties and Vickers took them over and proceeded to build the estate on the lines of Port Sunlight (the pioneering village of the Lever Brothers on the Wirral). Between 1899 and 1904 nearly 4,000 houses, a bowling green, an institute reading room and a park were constructed.

The streets were spacious but cheaply built, with pebble-dash render and timber-framed gables being a common feature. The site also lacked the landscaping of Port Sunlight.

The streets were named after ships built at Barrow and after famous admirals. Many are still maintained with pride and hence the Conservation Area accolade. The area behind the school, in particular, is well worth a visit with its Powerfull and Melamphis Streets.

The island is linked from Vickerstown to the mainland by Jubilee Bridge. Opened in 1908 as a toll bridge, and freed from this imposition in 1935, the structure was built to replace the ferry which served the then growing settlement of Vickerstown. The structure is, in part, a swing bridge but large vessels rarely use this upper part of Walney Channel nowadays. Replacement of the bridge is a matter of time – it is showing its age.

# Barrow-in Furness

At first sight, Barrow hardly appears to be an ideal place for a ramble, and even less so for a theme walk or a long distance footpath. The doyen of early Lake District walkers, M.J.B. Baddeley, set an early picture of the town when he wrote "Barrow is built on a dead flat, and has, though a well built modern town, nothing to attract the tourist, unless it be large docks and a fine town hall". This view is often repeated by modern guide book writers and comedians – but it deserves better than this. Maxwell Fraser came nearer the truth when she wrote "The name of Barrow-in-Furness is to many people a synonym for all that is dreary – most unjustly, for there are many less pleasant places.".

There are gems of history, of nature and fine views to be held at this town surrounded on three sides by seaside and beaches. It is also accessible, especially by rail, it offers accommodation and more than enough to hold the attention.

Once, Barrow and Furness were a detached part of Lancashire but since 1974 they form the southernmost tip of the huge county of Cumbria – a strain on allegiances was produced in the upheavals of local government reorganisation.

The name of the town is taken from Barrow Island, which is believed to be the site of a Norse burial ground. Today the island is the land between Walney Channel and Buccleugh Dock and largely occupied by VSEL, whose huge submarine building hall dominates the skyline for miles around. At the end of the eighteenth century the village of Barrowhead had around 300 souls but all changed following the building of three jetties to ship out Furness iron ore. With the help of local landowners, whose names are still to be recognised on local place names, and Henry Schneider – a speculator and dealer in iron – all was to change.

The coming of the Furness Railway in 1846 gave an impetus to the development, especially through the work of their locomotive superintendent James Ramsden. In 1850 Schneider was involved in a last ditch attempt to discover commercial quantities of iron ore and stumbled over the vast Park deposits. By 1857 the railway had become connected to the main London-Glasgow route and some local blast furnaces had been erected. Following this rise in local prosperity around this time, Ramsden began to plan a new town for Barrow.

The first major dock, the Devonshire, opened in 1867 (The Duke of Devonshire, like Buccleuch, was a major landowner). Barrow grew rapidly and some thought it was perhaps aiming to become a second Liverpool. Both landowners backed Ramsden's plan, which intended to concentrate industrial land adjacent to the docks and to locate housing areas further inland, linked by wide, tree lined streets.

By 1876 the ironworks claimed the title of the world's largest and another local industry, shipbuilding, had begun a few years earlier – a tradition on which the prosperity of Barrow still obviously depends.

Now, although the ironworks have gone, the slagbank still dominates the town's northern seaboard. Industry has diversified – the gas terminal from the Morecambe Bay field, toilet tissue, chemicals . . . but it is ships, especially submarines, which provide the economic barometer of the town's health.

## Barrow Town Trail

The Strand was intended to be the town centre in Ramsden's plan; to your right is the original railway station of 1846-50 and almost opposite were the offices of the Furness Railway Company. The bonded warehouse fronting onto Devonshire dock is a massive piece of mid nineteenth-century architecture.

St. George's church nearby is one of the few buildings in Barrow made from Lakeland green slate. The south chapel is called the Ramsden Chapel.

Just down to the right, if you came by Salthouse Road, lies a small terrace of cottages built for railway workers in local red sandstone in 1846. When they were constructed they increased the number of houses in Barrow by about 25% !

*Return down the Strand to Michaelson Road and then Schneider Square – with its statue of Schneider. Turning right you follow Dalton Road right through the shopping centre to arrive at Abbey Road. If you turn to the right, and then first left, you come to the modern day railway station built following bomb damage in the war.*

The original building on this site was Swiss styled and dated to 1884. Gone also from its glass cage on the platform is the old Furness Railway engine 'Coppernob', which, regretably, now rests on 'foreign' rails in the National Railway Museum in York.

If you turn left and delay your departure from the railway, go down Abbey Road – one of the tree lined streets of Ramsden's planned town – you look towards the massive covered shipyard, the home of Trident-carrying and other submarines. We pass the series of solid, individual structures that give a feeling of grandeur to the streets of Barrow – the bath house, technical college, Conservative Club and, at Ramsden Square, the library and museum. The latter is worth a short visit before continuing down Duke Street.

The statue of Ramsden (by Noble, 1872) has an interesting plaque depicting the industrial foundation of the town. Duke Street continues to show early and largely unaltered parts of the town's grid-pattern streets of terraced houses. Duke Street itself has some pleasant examples of moulded brickwork of the 1860s and 70s above shop level.

The terraces of houses close to the town centre gives Barrow's residents an opportunity to live close to the central amenities and, unlike many uninhabited town centres of the north-west, still gives a soul to the town. The terraces to the rear of the shops on the right of Duke Street are especially good examples of nineteenth-century artisans' dwellings with a more generous street width than many other back-to-back developments.

The Town Hall, where you can buy several useful publications on the natural history and architectural heritage of Barrow, was completed in 1882 and is designed to simulate classic thirteenth-century Gothic lines and is crowned with a high clock tower. The symmetry is spoiled by the council chamber having four windows. Tours of the town hall are sometimes available. Do not miss the stained glass window or the climb to the tower.

The main entrance, a porte cochere, is at the rear of the building, giving the hall an inverted feeling. Inside the red sandstone and slate roofed building some corners have an almost Dickensian atmosphere.

*Outside we are back at Schneider Square but, from outside the Town Hall a bus can be caught to Furness Abbey if time did not permit an earlier visit or you can return to the railway station.*

Check also if Barrow's Maritime Museum is open.

## Postscript

That concludes our description of the Cistercian Way. That may be the end; alternatively, it may well be the beginning of a long acquaintance. It may also serve to whet the appetite for the Cumbria Coastal Way, the guide to which is due for publication soon.

The countryside outside the Lake District National Park may not be as dramatic in scale or size, but it has its own charms. By following the Cistercian Way, you will readily appreciate many of its attractions and discover much that is of great and abiding interest.

I trust that you have had some enjoyment from your walk and, like me, you will return again and again to this unique, quiet and secret corner of the English countryside.

*Above: Cartmel Priory*

# Bibliography

Please note that some of these books are out of print and that some are collectors' pieces.

Barnes F., *Barrow and District*, Barrow Borough Council.
Barrow-in-Furness Borough Council, Heritage Trails, The Council.
Cartmel Priory Church, *Official Guide.*
Clare, Tom, *Archaeological Sites of the Lake District*, Moorland.
Conishead Priory, *Official Guide.*
Foulds, Elfrida, *Swarthmoor Hall Guide*, Quaker Home Services.
*Hampsfell Nature Trail*, Grange and District Natural History Society.
Hindle, Paul, *Roads and Trackways of the Lake District*, Moorland.
Holker Hall and Gardens, *Official Guide.*
Knapp-Fisher, H.C., *Furness and Cartmel*, St. Catherine.
Leach, Alice, *Furness Abbey*, Furness Heritage Press.
Millward, Roy & Robinson, Adrian, *Cumbria*, Macmillan.
Nicholson, Norman, *Greater Lakeland*, Hale.
Palmer, Willliam, *The Verge of Western Lakeland*, Hale.
Parker, John, *Cumbria*, Bartholomew.
Pevsner, Nikolaus, *North Lancashire* (Buildings of England Series), Penguin.
Robinson, Cedric, *One Man's Morecambe Bay*, Dalesman.
Robinson, Cedric & Mitchell Bill, *Life Around Morecambe Bay*, Dalesman.
Robinson, Huberta, *Walney Past and Present*, Archaeological Associates.
Rollinson William, *A History of Man in the Lake District*, Dent.
Trescatheric, Bryn, *Walney: A Wall in the Sea*, Hougenai Press.
Ulverston Civic Society, *Looking Around Ulverston*, U.C.S.
West, Thomas, *The Antiquities of Furness.*
West, Thomas, *Guide to the Lakes.*
*Westfields Nature Trails Guide*, Barrow Council.
Wordsworth, William, *The Poems* (2 vols), Penguin.

# Useful Addresses and Contacts

Barrow-in-Furness Borough Council,
Tourism and Planning Departments,
Town Hall, Duke Street, Barrow-in-
Furness, Cumbria, LA14 2LD.
Tel Barrow 25500

British Gas,
Rampside Terminal,
Barrow-in-Furness.

Alf Butler,
(Guide to the Leven Sands
Crossing):
Leven House, Canal Foot, Ulverston,
Cumbria, LA12 9EL.
Tel Ulverston 54156

Friends of the Lake District:
Yard 77, Highgate, Kendal, Cumbria,
LA9 4ED.

Holker Hall:
Flookburgh (044 853) 328.

South Lakeland Council,
Tourism Department and Footpath
Sections,
Stricklandgate House, Kendal,
Cumbria, LA9 4QQ.
Tel Kendal 33333.

Tourist Information Centres:

Barrow-in-Furness:
  Duke Street, Barrow.
  Tel Barrow 25795  *0229*

Grange-over-Sands:
  Main Street, Grange.
  Tel Grange-over-Sands 4026.

Ulverston:
  Coronation Hall, Ulverston.
  Tel Ulverston 57120.  *0229*

Swarthmoor Hall:
  Mrs Noble (Warden) at the Hall.
  Tel Ulverston 53204

Swarthmoor Meeting House:
  Mr Pye, 4 Meeting House Lane,
  Ulverston or the caretakers at 4
  Rakehead Cottages (by Meeting
  House Lane).

## Observe the Country Code

Enjoy the countryside and respect its life and work.
Guard against all risk of fire.
Fasten all gates.
Keep your dogs under close control.
Keep to public paths across farmland.
Use gates and stiles to cross fences, hedges and walls.
Leave livestock, crops and machinery alone.
Take your litter home.
Help to keep all water clean.
Protect wildlife, plants and trees.
Take special care on country roads.
Make no unnecessary noise.

Whilst the routes described in this guide follow definitive rights of way, we would request that walkers respect the privacy of local residents and refrain from straying off footpaths or otherwise trespassing on private property.

The publishers can take no responsibility for accident, damage, inconvenience or nuisance however caused. Walkers are urged to use the relevant Ordnance Survey Pathfinder Series maps for fine navigation and to identify the exact routes of footpaths.